]

A F

IONA

A Pilgrim's Guide

Peter W. Millar

Illustrated by
Gordon Menzies

Photography by
Martin Guppy

CANTERBURY
PRESS
Norwich

All biblical quotations are taken from the Good News Bible.

Text © Peter W. Millar 1997, 2007
Illustrations © Gordon Menzies
Photographs © Martin Guppy

First published in 1997 by The Canterbury Press Norwich
(a publishing imprint of Hymns Ancient & Modern Limited,
a registered charity)
St Mary's Works, St Mary's Plain,
Norwich, Norfolk NR3 3BH

This edition first published in 2007

British Library Cataloguing in Publication Data

A catalogue record for this book is available
from the British Library

978 1 85311 810 4

Printed and bound in the European Union

For the villagers of Iona
who welcome many pilgrims

Iona from Fionnphort

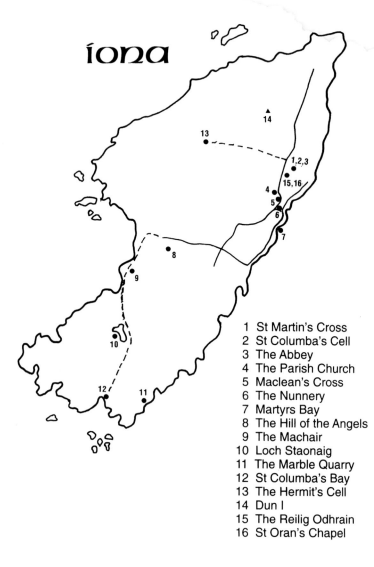

íona

1 St Martin's Cross
2 St Columba's Cell
3 The Abbey
4 The Parish Church
5 Maclean's Cross
6 The Nunnery
7 Martyrs Bay
8 The Hill of the Angels
9 The Machair
10 Loch Staonaig
11 The Marble Quarry
12 St Columba's Bay
13 The Hermit's Cell
14 Dun I
15 The Reilig Odhrain
16 St Oran's Chapel

Contents

An Introduction to Iona

I have heard modern Iona dismissed by its detractors simply as a mecca for 'spiritual tourism'. It is true that many of those who make the short crossing from Mull probably fall into the category of tourists but there is a very thin dividing line between tourism and pilgrimage. Among the island's visitors are many bearing pain or troubled with doubts and anxieties – contemporary pilgrims and penitents reaching out for healing and wholeness.

Ian Bradley

More than 1,400 years after Columba's death, Iona remains a place of pilrimage for people from every corner of the world. Iona or Columba's Isle (I Chalium Cille) is a sacred place permeated with the prayers and hopes of so many through the centuries; a place of holiness and healing, but also one of challenge and of new beginnings; a place where all may feel at home and accepted in God's love.

Iona's history, however, reaches much further back than the time of Columba. Geologists tell us that the rocks on Iona are around 2,700 million years old, a distant past which is beyond our imagining. Within human history, perhaps four to five thousand years before the coming of Christ, hunter gatherers roamed this and other Western Isles. Unworked flints from Mesolithic times have been unearthed in excavations near the Abbey, and it seems probable that communities working the land were on the island around 3500 BC.

The standing stones which are a feature of the Mull landscape are not found on Iona, although there are records of a Bronze Age burial cairn from the second millennium before

1

Christ. North-west of the Machair (the common grazing ground on the west side of the island) you can see a remnant of the ramparts of a small Iron Age hill-fort used by northern tribes speaking a Celtic language.

These Celtic peoples, who initially had had their roots in the region north of the Alps during the early centuries of the last millennium before the Christian era, have left an enduring legacy, although it is not one which we must over-romanticize. Certainly, their daily lives were pervaded by a sense of the supernatural; this power was often perceived to be malevolent and had to be contained through ritual and sacrifice. Numerous deities had to be appeased. The priests and divinators who occupied a central place within society were known as druids. There is no hard evidence to suggest that Iona was a druid centre, although later records speak of the island as 'The Isle of Druids'.

What we do know is that life for the Celts was always precarious – marked by daily struggles with the elements, illness and multiple hardships. Iona was a wild place, battered by strong winds and restless tides. When Columba and his fellow monks landed on the day of Pentecost in 563, the island was a rugged place in every sense – perhaps especially attractive to one whom we now recognize as both a penitent and a pilgrim.

With the monks' arrival, a new and extraordinary chapter in the island's long history had opened, a history which continues to unfold as we ourselves walk the pilgrim path, aware that the living God is always a God of surprises.

Every day is a messenger of God.

Russian proverb

The Iona Community

The Iona Community is an ecumenical Christian community, founded in 1938 by the late George MacLeod (the Very Revd Lord MacLeod of Fuinary). It is committed to seeking new ways of living the Gospel in today's world. Gathered around the restored ancient monastic buildings of Iona Abbey, but with its original inspiration in the poorest areas of Glasgow during the Depression, the Community has, since its inception, sought the 'rebuilding of the common life', bringing together work and worship, prayer and politics, the sacred and the secular.

Today, the Iona Community is a movement of around 200 members, over 1,400 Associate Members and about 1,600 Friends. The members – men and women from many backgrounds and denominations, most based in Britain but some overseas – are committed to a Common Rule of daily prayer and Bible study, sharing and accounting for the use of time and money, regular meetings and action for justice and peace.

In their work, corporately and individually, members pursue concerns of the Community relating to many areas: discovering new and relevant approaches to worship; promoting peace and social justice; supporting the cause of the poor and the exploited in Britain and abroad; political activity in combating racism; engagement with environmental and constitutional issues; commitment to strengthening interdenominational understanding and the sharing of Communion; the rediscovery of an integral approach to spirituality; the promotion of inter-faith dialogue and the development of the ministry of healing.

The members of the Community meet each other regularly throughout the year in local monthly Family Groups and in Plenary gatherings (the latter being held three times a year on the mainland, and for one week in the summer on Iona itself).

Through resident staff, with the assistance of seasonal volunteers, the Community maintains two centres on Iona (Iona Abbey, and the MacLeod Centre) and one on the Ross of Mull – the Camas Adventure Camp. These centres provide hospitality, as well as an opportunity to extend horizons and forge relationships through sharing an experience of the common life in worship, work, discussion and relaxation.

There can be no gospel of individual salvation without reference to the justice of the kingdom. There is no love of God unrelated to my neighbour.

Emilio Castro

O Christ, the Master Carpenter
Who, at the last, through wood and nails,
Purchased our whole salvation,
Wield well your tools in the workshop of
your world,
So that we, who come rough-hewn to your bench,
May here be fashioned to a truer beauty of
your hand.
We ask it for your own name's sake.
The Iona Community Worship Book

A Pilgrimage around Iona

Every Tuesday, from March to October, the Iona Community organizes a pilgrimage around Iona, in which everyone is welcome to join. Beginning at 10.15 a.m. at St Martin's Cross (in front of the Abbey), and ending in St Oran's Chapel around 3.30 p.m., the pilgrimage visits places of historical and religious significance on the island. It is a wonderful opportunity to reflect on the journey of your life, and the life of God's world. At each station there is a brief reflection and prayer, and sometimes silence or songs. Parts of the route are also walked in silence. A cup of tea is provided for all pilgrims at around one o'clock; and, if they wish, pilgrims may complete only part of the walk.

Although Tuesday is the 'official' pilgrimage day, the paths are freely available for you to walk on any day you choose. Whatever the day of the week on which you make your pilgrimage, we hope that this guide will enrich your time, enabling you to learn a little more about each station, as well as offering prayers and thoughts for reflection and meditation.

Even if your feet are sore when you arrive at St Oran's Chapel, may your heart be rested.

Practical tips

As we journey, it is good to remember that farming and crofting are integral parts of life for the local community, and that various gates must be left as they are found (either open or closed).

Litter should be kept until a refuse bin is sighted. The pilgrim route is often rough and wet underfoot, so strong footwear and waterproof clothing are highly recommended.

If you love me, you will obey my commandments. I will ask the Father, and he will give you another Helper, who will stay with you for ever. He is the Spirit who reveals the truth about God. The world cannot receive him, because it cannot see him or know him. But you know him, because he remains with you and is in you.

John 14: 15–17

In every person it is possible to see Christ's own face. Nothing has more beauty than a face that a whole life of struggle has rendered transparent.

Brother Roger of Taizé

Bless to us, O God,
The earth beneath our feet,
Bless to us, O God,
The path whereon we go,
Bless to us, O God,
The people whom we meet.

Based on an old prayer from the Outer Hebrides

IONA

1

St Martin's Cross

This magnificent cross has stood on Iona for over a thousand years. It is named after Hungarian-born St Martin, a fourth-century Roman soldier who, one cold winter night, sliced his military cloak (*capella*) down the middle and gave it to a disabled person. Shortly after, he had a vision of Christ and the direction of his life was totally changed. He was baptized, and became known for his conscientious objection to serving in the Roman army. Later, as Bishop of Tours, he played an important role in the mission to the Celts, although he never visited Britain. Martin died in 397 at the age of eighty and was buried on 11 November, a day which centuries later would be associated with peace-making and reconciliation.

Iona possesses the remains of five ancient High Crosses, but only this cross is complete and standing on its original site. Close to it is the modern replica of St John's Cross and the remains of St Matthew's Cross. (The original St John's Cross, along with the remains of two other crosses, is in the Abbey museum.)

This group of crosses marked a place of great spiritual significance: probably the site of Columba's grave as well as an ancient church building. Adomnan, who became the ninth Abbot of Iona in 682 and who wrote the famous *Life of Columba*, speaks of their purpose as sacred markers. Sometimes they were erected at sites – such as the entrance to a burial ground – which were considered to be cosmic entrance and exit points, areas where the material and spiritual world came into especially close contact.

High Crosses were erected in the tradition of the tall menhirs or standing stones of the pre-Christian period, and their intricately carved designs, rich in symbolism, fused Christian and pre-Christian motifs. Worship was held

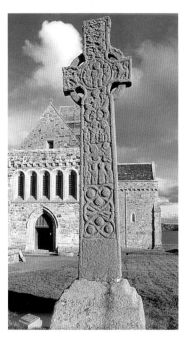

St Martin's Cross

around them and they were also places for penitential exercises.

St Martin's Cross is a solid block of epediorite. Originally it had wooden or granite extensions fitting into the slots on the two side arms. On its west face, in the centre, the Virgin and Child can be seen; carved down the shaft are several Old Testament scenes such as Daniel in the lion's den and David playing the harp. On its east face, the carving is ornamental, with prominent jewel-like bosses. Scholars have suggested that the characteristic ring, which is such a prominent feature of Celtic crosses, originated on Iona and then spread to Ireland.

The vibrant Celtic pattern of the weaving vine points to the intertwining of heaven and earth. George MacLeod reflected on this when he said that Iona itself was a 'thin-place' where the material and spiritual came close to each other. On our pilgrimage today we look at the spiritual at the heart of the physical world.

We have to recognise in a spirit of true humility and penance that the church has not always been faithful to its prophetic mission, to its evangelical role in being in solidarity with the people. Yet at every moment, the living Word of God is sent to the church inviting it to return to the fervour and vision of the first disciples.

Church statement from north-east Brazil

May you come to know Christ's love, although it can never be fully known, and so be filled with the very nature of God.

Ephesians 3:19

Consider every day that you are for the first time – as it were – beginning: and always act with the same fervour as on the first day you began.

St Anthony of Padua

From the cowardice that dare not face new truth,
From the laziness that is content with half truth,
From the arrogance that thinks it knows all truth,
Good Lord, deliver us.

Prayer from Kenya

Let go: let God

Church poster

2

St Columba's Cell

Close to St Martin's Cross is the small hillock known as Tor Abb. On the top, stone foundations for the walls of a bee-hive-shaped cell were uncovered in 1957. This may have been Columba's cell; he may also have had a second cell on wooden foundations which he used for writing. Beside the cell is a socket for a cross: this is probably medieval.

Those who trust in the Lord for help
will find their strength renewed.
They will rise on wings like eagles;
they will run and not get weary;
they will walk and not grow weak.

Isaiah 40:31

Everybody can be great. Because anybody can serve. You don't have to have a college degree to serve. You don't have to know about Plato and Aristotle to serve. You don't have to know Einstein's theory of relativity to serve. You only need a heart full of grace. A soul generated by love.

Martin Luther King

The Monastery Buildings

Standing on Tor Abb, and looking down at the Abbey and Cloistral buildings, try to imagine what the Columba settlement was like. There were none of the buildings you see before you; instead small beehive-shaped cells made of timber and turf would have stood on the ground below you. There would have been a small rectangular church and other public buildings, such as the guest house and refectory. All these would be inside a boundary wall (the vallum) and beyond would lie farm buildings and ground cultivated by the monks. Work and worship in those days were inseparable.

None of these structures survive, but the vallum can be seen – running north to the west of the main road, then turning east across the field to the north of the Abbey. The vallum, a rectangle of land measuring approximately 1,100 feet by 500 feet, delimited the monastic enclosure rather than serving as a defensive structure.

Columba and his monks established their monastery in 563, the year of their arrival. From there they conducted a mission to the Picts in the north, to the Anglo-Saxons in Northumbria, and throughout Europe, reaching as far east as western Russia. During the next two centuries, under a series of abbots (many of whom were related to Columba), the monastic buildings were frequently rebuilt.

At the end of the eighth century, the west coast of Scotland was ravaged by a series of Viking raids and settled monastic life became impossible. The monks left the island in the middle of the ninth century and moved to the safety of the monastery at Kells, Ireland, which took over the leadership of the Columba 'family' of monasteries. Later a small community returned to Iona and built in stone, but the Viking threat was such that the rebuilt monastery was not very large.

The Abbey from Tor Abb

Your word is a lamp to guide me
and a light for my path.

Psalm 119:105

I read in a book that a man called Christ went about
doing good. It was very disconcerting to me that I am
so easily satisfied with just going about.

Toyohiko Kagawa of Japan

God our Father, who gave to your servant Columba
the gifts of courage, faith and cheerfulness, and sent
people forth from Iona to carry the word of your
gospel to every creature, grant we pray, a like spirit to
your church even at this present time. Further in all
things the purpose of our community, that hidden
things may be revealed to us, and new ways found to
touch the hearts of all.

The Iona Community Worship Book

13

The Abbey Church (St Mary's Cathedral)

The Benedictine Abbey was founded by Reinald, son of Somerled, Lord of the Isles, in 1203. The close links between the Abbey and the Lords of the Isles (a title now held by the Prince of Wales) and its freedom from episcopal jurisdiction, gave the Abbot of Iona an important role in the medieval Church. Throughout the following four centuries the Abbey derived its revenues from lands and parish churches on the islands of Iona, Mull, Colonsay, Oronsay, Tiree, Islay, Skye and Uist, and on the mainland. It was a small monastery compared with the greater religious houses of Scotland, but the association of the island with Columba gave it a certain pre-eminence. Around 1420, extensive rebuilding took place, with the tower and choir being completely re-modelled.

Before the Reformation in 1560, however, the lands of the Abbey had begun to decrease and religious life had declined. After the Reformation, the church was used by the Bishop of the Isles (now Protestant), but in 1693 it came into the possession of the Argyll family. By the nineteenth century, the Abbey buildings were in a ruinous state. In 1874, the eighth Duke of Argyll began work to strengthen the walls of the church, making them safe enough to support a new roof. He realized that he would not be able to complete the restoration of the church in his lifetime, and so in 1899 he donated the Abbey, together with other sacred buildings of Iona, to the Iona Cathedral Trustees, who remain responsible for the upkeep of the buildings to this day.

The Duke of Argyll set two conditions on his gift. Firstly, that the Abbey church should be restored as a place of worship and not merely as a museum for tourists, and secondly, that it should be a home for Christians of all denominations.

By 1910, through public subscription, the Abbey church had been gloriously restored.

Entering the Abbey church by the west door, one is immediately struck by the simple beauty of the interior. Although only fragments remain of the thirteenth-century structure, later additions and restorations have been harmonious, even though they have been spread over many centuries. Several stone coffins were discovered beneath the nave during the 1899–1910 restoration. Two of these coffins contained small stones (which you can see cemented in circles in the floor), perhaps indicating the number of years these particular monks had served in the Order.

The eastern end of the church dates from the fifteenth-century rebuilding. In medieval times, the choir contained the stalls for the monks and its roof would have been flat, just as the nave roof is now.

Close to the beautiful sacristy door is the fine effigy of John MacKinnon, last Abbot of Iona, who died around 1499.

15

The effigy on the south side of the presbytery is almost certainly that of Dominic, Abbot from 1421–65. Beside it within the wall itself is the fifteenth-century sedilia – the seats on which the celebrants of High Mass would have sat.

The Communion Table is made of marble from Iona; behind it there is a cross created by Omar Ramsden. The oak screen in the north transept was gifted by the Queen in 1956, and the south transept contains a monument to the eighth Duke of Argyll, and the tomb of his wife.

In a corner close to the west door is a small cell called the 'Porter's Watch'. This would have served a practical function. A monk would sit in the cell and look out through its window onto the Street of the Dead, to see if anyone was approaching. By the time of their arrival, a welcome would have been prepared – hospitality was an important feature of monastic life.

St Columba's Shrine is the name given to the small chapel (originally thought to be free-standing) that is sited to the north of the west door. There is evidence of medieval burials beneath its floor; it may even be possible that this is the original site of Columba's grave. Certainly, the positioning of the High Crosses nearby suggests that this was a place of great importance. Columba's bones were taken for safe keeping to Kells in 849, although some relics may have been brought back to Iona at a later date. The magnificent Book of Kells which is now housed at Trinity College, Dublin, was probably begun by the monks on Iona between 790 and 830 and taken to Kells a few years later.

Today, the Cathedral Trustees, their business subsidiary Iona Abbey Ltd and the Iona Community all work in close co-operation to ensure that the Abbey church is maintained both as a historical building and as a place of daily Christian worship. It is hardly an exaggeration to say that this rebuilt Benedictine Abbey is one of the great works of restoration in Britain in the twentieth century.

'I am telling you the truth,' said Jesus. 'No one can enter the Kingdom of God unless they are born of water and the Spirit. A person is born physically of human parents, but they are born spiritually of the Spirit. Do not be surprised because I tell you that you must be born again. The wind blows where it wishes: you hear the sound it makes, but you do not know where it comes from or where it is going. It is like that with everyone who is born of the Spirit.'

John 3:5–8

God always approaches us from beneath and we must stoop to meet him.

Nicholas Zernov

Lord, may we recognize that the real sanctity of this restored church is that it is a sacred place where we can go to weep and laugh in common, renewed and forgiven in your enfolding love and light.

17

5

The Cloistral Buildings

The Iona Community began the monumental task of rebuilding this part of the Abbey precincts in 1938, and with the support of friends around the world, the main work was finished by the mid 1960s. The actual physical rebuilding was in itself a symbol of the restoration of the common life in our local communities.

It is unusual to find the cloistral building of a monastery lying on the shaded north side of the church, but sanitation requirements dictated this arrangement: the stream which provided the water ran on the north side of the Abbey precincts.

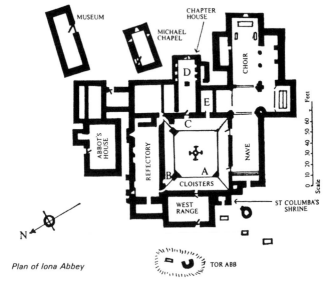

Plan of Iona Abbey

Cloistral Buildings

Only two pillars on the west side of the cloisters remain from the original Benedictine building. The tradition of sculpture, seen in the High Crosses and in the carvings in the church, is continued in the cloisters today. Carved on the pillars on the east side of the cloisters are plants of the Bible; on the north, plants of Iona; on the south, birds of Iona; and on the west, flowers of Britain. The corner capitals have distinct sculptures, and this work is ongoing.

The sculpture at the centre of the cloisters is called *The Descent of the Spirit*, and was given to the Abbey in the 1950s by the Lithuanian sculptor, Jacob Lipschitz. The inscription reads 'I a Jew, faithful to the faith of my fathers, have made this Virgin for goodwill among all people, that the Spirit may reign.' In the centre of the sculpture is Mary, who represents the highest being that nature can create. She holds out her hands in an offering to God, but she is blind. The lamb, representing human suffering, is also blind. Mary is supported by three angels, above her is the dove and around her is the Holy Spirit. The Spirit takes away our blindness, and through our new vision we see the world as God's creation. As a whole it represents the Incarnation, the lamb becoming the Lamb of God.

The cloisters are enclosed by the West Range, the Refectory and the East Range. The latter now houses Abbey guests. All the timber in the restored Refectory was a gift from Norway. To the north of the Refectory lies a building which was probably the Abbot's House; this is linked to the cloistral buildings by the reredorter. The reredorter contained the latrines in the Benedictine period but is now the Abbey warden's home!

To the east of the main cloistral buildings lie two rectangular buildings now restored from their foundations. The date of these is uncertain. It was usual for essential buildings which were not connected with the disciplined life of the monastery, such as the infirmary and its chapel, to be situated here. These buildings may have served this purpose. Now, however, the building to the south is the restored Michael Chapel in which the roof and stalls are made of utile wood from Ghana. The other building is a museum, restored as a result of the generosity of the Carnegie Trust. The stones in the museum represent work of the early Christian period as well as the schools of monumental sculpture which began on Iona around 1330 and lasted up to the Reformation.

Help us to carry one another's burdens, and in this way you will obey the law of Christ.

Galatians 6:2

The cloisters have always been the place of 'common life' where barriers are broken down and our true humanity, in Christ, is discovered. Here we recognize our essential inner connectedness in God's love and are challenged anew to accept 'the other' who may be very different from us.

Across the barriers that divide race from race;
Across the barriers that divide rich from poor;
Across the barriers that divide people of different faiths;
Across the barriers that marginalize so many;
Come Lord,
And reconcile us through your pain and tears
For all the world.

6

Between the Abbey and the Nunnery

After passing the St Columba Hotel with its magnificent garden, we come to the parish church. The church, which is part of the national Presbyterian Church of Scotland, was built in 1828 under Thomas Telford and was renovated in 1939. It was one of a series of 'Parliamentary kirks' erected under a government scheme to increase the number of churches in the Highlands. Fifty years previously, in 1774, the Scottish Society for the Propagation of Christian Knowledge had established a village school.

Adjacent to the church is the Manse. In recent years this fine house has been divided into two parts. The upper floor provides a flat for the minister, while the ground-floor rooms have been converted into an exceptionally attractive Heritage Centre. This is an initiative of the local community and much care has been taken over the exhibits.

Close to the parish church stands Maclean's Cross, which dates from the last years of the fifteenth century. In medieval times three streets met here. On the front of the cross is a representation of the crucified Saviour, while the shaft is decorated with the familiar and beautiful intertwining Celtic pattern. The cross was a product of the Iona school of sculpture and was probably commissioned by the Macleans of Duart and Lochbuie, the most influential family in the district at that time.

Approaching the Nunnery, you can see a small stone monument on the left-hand side of the road. The inscription reminds us of how in 1979 the island was purchased from the Argyll family by the Hugh Fraser Foundation and subsequently given into the care of the National Trust of Scotland.

✠

The real atheism is to exclude God from our worldly concerns or to exclude the world from our religious concerns.

A Chinese Christian

Biblical faith is prophetically relevant to everything that happens in the world.

The Kairos Document, South Africa

Christ be beside me,
Christ be before me,
Christ be behind me,
King of my heart.
Christ be within me,
Christ be below me,
Christ be above me,
Never to part.

St Patrick

MacLean's Cross

22

7

The Nunnery

The Augustinian Nunnery, dedicated to St Mary the Virgin, was built in the thirteenth century, around the same time as the Benedictine Abbey (although there may have been an earlier one on the 'Island of Women' – Eilean nam Ban – opposite Iona). The Nunnery, known locally as 'The Black Church' (An Eaglais Dhubh), housed a religious community until the latter part of the sixteenth century.

Nearby is the re-roofed medieval parish church of St Ronan (Teampull Ronain) which was for centuries the place of worship for the local community. Close to St Ronan's is the ancient graveyard for women and children. From the medieval period onwards, at least in some areas, women and men were buried in different cemeteries and perhaps also worshipped in different churches.

As we stand within the beautiful ruins of the Nunnery, considered to be one of the best preserved examples of its kind in Britain, we can imagine the nuns worshipping in the nave of the little chapel, sharing meals in the refectory, meeting in the Chapter House and overseeing their lands south of Loch Staonaig. Yet although we can visualize these activities, there is little historical record of the life of the countless women who lived together in this place for over 300 years.

History has provided us with an almost total focus on the Abbey. This lack of historical attention to the Nunnery reflects the neglect of women in a society and Church of male domination. Hand in hand with the subordination of women has gone the neglect of the earth and an abuse of the human body.

These walls now remind us of all the silent and hidden women of history for whom we give thanks to God. They

The Nunnery

also speak to us of all the women who today are struggling for freedom and justice, often in places of poverty and exploitation.

One of the offerings of the Celtic Church is its greater balance between the feminine and the masculine, as well as its celebration of the intertwining of matter and spirit, and its affirmation of the goodness of creation. St Brigid, a great figure of the Celtic period, in her leadership of double monasteries of women and men, stands as a model of equality between the sexes.

Earlier in this century there were suggestions about rebuilding the Nunnery, but these plans never came to fruition. Today, with the enormous worldwide interest in sacred places, some would like to see these buildings restored. Yet the quiet and gentle beauty of the Nunnery precincts are much needed on Iona today, and in their present state they are a powerful witness to the Gospel, albeit in a different way from the rebuilt Abbey. In their ruined state, they remind us that much of our community life, especially in Western societies, lies in ruins; that the struggles for genuine equality between women and men have a long way to go, and that the cries of oppressed women, children and men around the world become louder with each new day.

Blessed is She who spoke and the world became.
Blessed is She who in the beginning gave birth.
Blessed is She who says and performs.
Blessed is She who declares and fulfils.
Blessed is She whose womb covers the earth.
Blessed is She who lives forever, and exists eternally.
Blessed is She who redeems and saves.
Blessed is Her name.

'Sabbath Prayer', Naomi Janowitz and Maggie Wenig

I know that it feels mighty strange to see a black woman get up and tell you about things. We have all been thrown down so low that nobody thought we'd ever get up again: but we have been long enough trodden now: we will come up again, and now I am here.

Sojourner Truth, speaking in New York in 1853

Let us dream. Let us prophesy. Let us see visions of love, peace and justice. Let us affirm with humility, with joy, with faith, with courage, that you, O Christ, are the life of every child, woman and man.

From South African women

8

The Village

Surrounding us as we leave the Nunnery is the village: the primary school, the doctor's surgery, the Carnegie Library which was opened in 1904, the village hall, the Post Office, shops and many private homes.

It is sometimes easy for a visitor to forget the central role of the local community, which numbers around ninety people. Iona is far more than a collection of sacred sites and ancient monuments. Through the generations, the island has been first and foremost a local community carrying the relationships and hopes of its people. It is a vibrant community, aware of its rich history, but also forward-looking.

Every year the islanders welcome thousands of people into the midst of their small community, and their hospitality is valued by individuals and families from every part of the world. Yet the local folk also face the difficulties and

hardships experienced by isolated rural communities – perhaps especially in the winter months when even travelling to Oban can take on the dimensions of a major expedition!

In addition to the National Trust of Scotland, several other public bodies have interests on the island, and the Iona Community Council is a forum through which local people can express their views.

Small rural communities have much to teach all of us. May we be able to listen with sensitivity to that collective wisdom at a time when we are fast discovering that 'bigger' is not always 'better'.

To become aware of the sacramental nature of the cosmos, to be open to the sacramental possibilities of each moment, to see the face of Christ in every person, these things are not novel, but their rediscovery is the beginning of our health.

Ron Ferguson

For partners who love,
For kids who cuddle,
For grannies who listen,
For friends who care;
For the stars above,
For food on the table,
For laughter and tears,
And for so much more,
We say 'Thanks'
To you,
Today and every day.

9

Martyrs Bay

Martyrs Bay, situated close to the village, has had an important role in the history of Iona and holds many memories.

In 806, the bay was a scene of violence when sixty-eight monks were mercilessly slaughtered at the hands of the Norse invaders. That violence reminds us of all victims of torture and massacre in our contemporary world, and the continuing task of reconciliation.

This bay is also hallowed for other reasons. Through the centuries it has provided a landing place for funeral processions. Here were carried ashore the mortal remains of kings and chiefs and many less-exalted folk. Their coffins rested on a grassy knoll called the 'Ealadh', before moving on to the final part of their journey to the Reilig Odhran (the graveyard).

North of the bay is the War Memorial which commemorates villagers who died while serving their country in war in this century. A part of Martyrs Bay was also a graveyard in earlier times.

> For I am certain that nothing can separate us from God's love: neither death nor life; neither the present nor the future; there is nothing in all creation that will ever be able to separate us from the love of God which is ours through Christ Jesus our Lord.
>
> *Romans 8:38–39*

> O God, give us your shielding,
> O God, give us your holiness,
> O God, give us your comfort
> And your peace at the hour of our death.
>
> *Celtic traditional*

10

The Hill of the Angels

To the left of the road as one approaches the gate into the Machair is a small hill known as the 'Hill of the Angels' (Cnoc nan Aingeal) where Columba is said to have met with a 'multitude of angels'. The account of this meeting is dramatically described in Adomnan's *Life of Columba*:

> The Blessed man was standing on a certain knoll, praying with outstretched hands and with his eyes raised to heaven. Then, with marvellous suddenness, holy angels, citizens of the heavenly country, flew down and began to stand about the holy man as he prayed. After some converse with the blessed man, that heavenly throng quickly returned to the highest heaven.

For the pre-Christian Celt, the world was full of spirits, fairies and demons, many of which took on physical shape and revealed themselves in ordinary life. It is not without significance that this little hill's other Gaelic name is 'Sitheon Mor' – the 'Fairy Hill'.

However, we must be careful to guard against Adomnan's account of the saint's meeting with the angels as merely reflecting a pre-Christian world-view. The Early Church was powerfully aware of supernatural beings, as were the writers of both the Old and New Testaments.

Down through the centuries, in the Christian tradition, there has always been an awareness of angels, even if sometimes their activity was down-played. Many traditional Celtic prayers speak unself-consciously of angels, and today in the churches there is renewed interest in the ministry of angels.

The Lord is your defender and protector. No disaster will strike you, and no violence will come near your home. God will put his angels in charge of you to protect you wherever you go. They will hold you up with their hands to keep you from hurting your feet on the stones.

Psalm 91:9–12

Thou angel of God who has charge of me,
Drive me from every temptation and danger;
And in the narrows, crooks and straits,
Keep thou my coracle, keep it always.
Celtic traditional

The Machair

11

The Machair

The Machair (which means 'raised beach'), is the common grazing ground on the west side of the island overlooking the 'Bay at the Back of the Ocean'. It was used for agriculture by the Celtic monks and later as a cornfield by the Benedictines.

Today it is a field used by the local farmers and crofters for grazing, and also by others as a golf course, kept in immaculate condition by the resident sheep! In August this amazing golf course plays host to an annual competition with players coming from far and wide.

Port Ban is a wonderfully sheltered cove just to the north of the Machair, while closer is the famous 'Spouting Cave' where the force of the waves, in rough weather, sends a plume of water over a hundred feet high into the air.

At all times of the year, the Machair is a place of great natural beauty and peace. It is humanly and spiritually a significant place in the landscape, and because of the co-operative way in which it is used, is itself a parable of sharing, of community.

It is on this fertile soil, the place of sharing, that we who are contemporary pilgrims in an increasingly privatized society, stop for lunch on our return from Columba's Bay – eating together and giving thanks to God for all his blessings. Here we are challenged to share our gifts and talents, to work for global justice and to care for the earth.

We walk across the Machair in silence, reflecting on the ways in which we can personally act to preserve our environments from further destruction. We also think about the crofting way of life, integral to Iona's social fabric, and carrying an inner wisdom and awareness forgotten in much of modern farming.

For centuries, far too many Christians have presumed that God's love is primarily directed at them, and that his natural order was created mainly for the use, and abuse, of humankind. Today such a human-centred attitude to our fragile and exhausted planet is at last beginning to look not only selfish and parochial, but also irresponsible and potentially dangerous. Hence all of us must open our eyes and minds wider still. We must realize that the way to maintain the value and preciousness of the human is by reaffirming the preciousness of the non-human also – of all that is. Indeed, the Christian God forbids the idea of a cheap creation, of a finite, disposable universe. God's universe is a work of non-expendable and ever-renewing love – and nothing that is fashioned in love must ever be regarded as cheap or secondary.

Robert Runcie, former Archbishop of Canterbury

Enjoy the earth gently,
Enjoy the earth gently;
For if the earth is spoiled
it cannot be repaired.
Enjoy the earth gently.

Yoruba poem, West Africa

Teach us, Lord, to walk the soft earth as relatives of all that live.

Native American prayer

12

Loch Staonaig

Loch Staonaig means 'the rocky pool' and until recently it was the island's primary water supply – peat coloured and high in mineral content. However, by modern standards it was not an abundant supply and Iona's water now comes across the sea (or rather beneath it) from Mull. Yet for many of our sisters and brothers in the world the water here would be more than miraculously plentiful.

In the pre-Christian Celtic religion, rivers and lochs were seen as dwelling places of divinities, and springs and wells as sacred areas with healing properties. The Celts associated wells with particular saints, and the sea played a significant role in the spirituality of Columba and his fellow monks. St Cuthbert actually waded into the North Sea off Lindisfarne to chant psalms, as did St David off the Pembrokeshire coast.

The Bible mentions water many times. In the Old Testament we read of the power of God moving across the face of the waters; in the New Testament, Jesus offers the Samaritan woman the 'water of life'. In Christian baptism, water signifies many dimensions of faith, and its symbolic nature within the churches is being more deeply valued as we revisit our Celtic heritage.

In the light of these separate strands of thought, our reflection here has various dimensions. On the one hand, we remember the sacred and healing nature of water – its life-giving potential. On the other, we recognize that water, through all of human history, has been a source of political conflict and war – and continues to be so today.

Even as we ourselves may feel comforted and inwardly assured that Christ brings us the 'water of life', we are – at the same time – unable to forget the fact that every day millions of God's children have to walk for miles to find even a single cup of water. Thus our heart is both disturbed and calmed as we gaze at the ever-changing beauty of this Highland loch.

Jesus said to the Samaritan woman, 'Whoever drinks the water from this well will be thirsty again, but whoever drinks the water that I will give them will never be thirsty again.'

John 4:13–14

Too long have I worried about so many 'things':
And yet, my Lord, few are needed!
May I today, live more simply
– like the bread
May I today, see more clearly
– like the water
May I today, be more selfless
– like the Christ.

Traditional Russian prayer

13

The Marble Quarry

The stone in the quarry is white in colour, streaked and mottled with yellowish-green serpentine. Quarrying on Iona by the Argyll Estates stopped around 1915, but here in the quarry we can see remains of a producer-gas engine, a cutting frame, a small rock-cut reservoir, a gun-powder store and a roughly built quay which provided the only means of transporting equipment and marble to and from the site. The round-angled, dry-stone building at the head of the gully was probably erected in the 1790s in connection with the operations of the short-lived Iona Marble company.

The first written reference to the quarry dates from 1693, but the veins were worked from a much earlier date, and it

The Marble Quarry

is possible that the Benedictines carved their high altar from here. The quarry also provided the present communion table and baptismal font in the Abbey. In Victorian times, the marble was used extensively in public buildings, churches and private homes both in this country and abroad.

Here we reflect on the situation in our world, where natural resources are being exploited and where human lives are being broken in the pursuit of wealth and power. We remember also the hidden workers of the world whose toil we often take for granted, and the local men who worked here – often under extremely harsh conditions. Situated above some of the oldest geological formations in Europe, the quarry reminds us of the earth's evolution over hundreds of millions of years and of our place in creation's unfolding. Human life seems so fleeting when measured against our planet's evolution. Yet each of us has a place within God's purposes. That is both our hope and the source of our compassion.

Lord, you set the mountains in place
by your strength:
you calm the roar of the seas
and the noise of the waves:
the whole world stands in awe
of your deeds,
of the great things you have done.
Your deeds bring shouts of joy
from one end of the earth to the other
and every hillside
declares your glory.

Adapted from Psalm 65

O God of the high heavens,
O Christ of the deep earth,
O Spirit of the flowing waters,
O Trinity of love,
You have offered your love to us,
And here we pledge our love to you.
You have been faithful to your people through the ages,
And here we pledge our faithfulness to one another.
You have sustained in love the earth, sea and sky
around us,
And here we pledge our sustaining love for creation.
You have identified with the powerless and the weak
of the world,
And here we pledge our identification with them.

O God, strengthen us in our desire,
And breathe into our bodies the passion of your love.
We pray this in the name of Jesus
To whom we commit ourselves.

The Iona Community Worship Book

Looking towards the south end of Iona

37

14

St Columba's Bay

On this pebbled beach at the southern tip of the island, Columba is said to have arrived from Ireland on the Day of Pentecost in 563. Legend has it that, having clambered up the beach with their leather-bound boat (known as a coracle), Columba and his twelve monks climbed the hill to the west of the bay to confirm that their beloved home country could not be seen. 'The Hill of the Back to Ireland' became a landmark for them as they moved forward in mission. There were many reasons behind Columba's departure from Ireland – political, spiritual and social. Artist, poet, politician, prophet, penitent and saint – Columba was all of these, and spent the last thirty-five years of his life on Iona in 'white martyrdom' – meaning a life spent in sacrifice.

Every part of Iona has a story, and this small bay – known as Port a'Churaich (the Harbour of the Curragh) – is steeped in legend. The Celts took a particular delight in immortaliz-

St Columba's Bay

38

ing even the most insignificant details of their human story; tiny hills, hidden coves, deep caves, broad beaches and special stones took on names that are descriptive of events and of individual achievements.

The story of Columba has been kept alive; the present, in a sense, becomes inseparably linked to the past, and in this sacred place we seek for new beginnings in our own life and for a deeper faith in Jesus, the Risen One. May we also move on from here committed to share the good news of the Gospel as Columba did many centuries before us; carrying and announcing the truth of Christ in our communities where many are seeking his light.

As part of our meditation at this bay we take two pebbles from the beach. One we throw into the sea as a symbol of something in our lives we would like to leave behind, while the other we take back with us as a sign of a new commitment in our heart.

> They pulled the boats up on the beach, left everything and followed Jesus.
>
> *Luke 5:11*

> God has created me to do him some definite service. He has committed some work to me which he has not committed to another. I have my mission. I may never know it in this world. But I shall be told it in the next.
>
> I am a link in the chain, a bond of connection between persons. I shall be a preacher of truth in my own place, while not intending it, if I but keep his commandments.
>
> Therefore will I trust him. Wherever, whatever I am, I can never be thrown away. He does nothing in vain. The Lord knows what he is about.
>
> *Cardinal John Newman*

Set our hearts on fire with love to thee, O Christ,
that in that flame we may love thee
and our neighbour as ourselves.

Eastern Orthodox prayer

Note to pilgrims

After leaving Columba's Bay, we retrace the route back to Loch Staonaig and thence downhill to the Machair. The route then goes straight across to the north end of the Machair where the boundary fence is crossed via a small wooden stile. We then head for the low-lying hills and walk through them in an easterly direction until another boundary fence is reached. The route then goes up over some high, rocky ground before descending steeply to another gate close to the Hermit's Cell.

NB. If you are not with a larger group, it is good to have a map for this part of the pilgrimage.

15

The Hermit's Cell

Now only a secluded ring of stones, situated towards the north of the island, the Gaelic name of the Hermit's Cell means 'secluded hollow'. Places of solitude were integral to Columban Christianity. There are many accounts of Columba spending time alone in prayer in various parts of Iona, and in the centuries that followed, the monks continued to build small cells for retreat purposes – as did the Augustinian nuns. Yet whether one was all alone in a cell or living in community, manual labour was obligatory. Both in the Columban and Benedictine traditions, contemplation and work were continually interconnected.

Tradition may have bestowed on this cell an exclusively religious use, although there are in other parts of the island similar stone foundations which were either temporary houses or enclosures for the cows. If this was a place that sheltered animals, rather than monks, it still has sacred significance. Over the centuries, the cow and her calf within the island's economy were truly rich gifts from the Creator's hand.

Whatever its history, this spot has welcomed the prayers and meditations of countless pilgrims, the silent longings of human hearts seeking assurance from the One who understands all our desires, and from whom no secrets are hidden.

We need times of solitude and silence to undergird the demands of each day. As well as hearing the word of God through Scripture, through creation and through one another, we can experience the mystery of God deep within us at the heart of our being.

The Hermit's Cell

Examine me, O God, and know my mind;
test me, and discover my thoughts.
Find out if there is any evil in me
and guide me in the everlasting way.

Psalm 139:23–24

Dear master, may thy light shine on me now, as it once shone on the shepherds as they kept their flocks by night.

Oszaki, a Japanese leprosy patient

We all seek for that Light in our own ways: often unconsciously. Our hearts are restless till we discover Christ's truth and make it our own. Yet Christ's transformation in our lives brings a new restlessness – what Helder Camara of Brazil called 'the uncomfortable peace of Jesus'. A peace that is strong and life-giving, for it brings to our lives a deeper compassion, a more informed awareness, and an understanding that God's strength can be found not only in some holy place such as Iona, but in the midst of life's daily contradictions and uncertainties.

> Deep peace of the running wave to you,
> Deep peace of the flowing air to you,
> Deep peace of the quiet earth to you,
> Deep peace of the shining stars to you,
> Deep peace of the Son of Peace to you.
>
> *Celtic blessing*

16

Dun I

Dun I viewed from the Sound

Dun I simply means 'hill of Iona' and at 332 feet above sea level it is the highest point on the island. No doubt you feel a great sense of achievement as you reach the stone cairn at its summit!

To the north, in the far distance and on a clear day, you can see the Cuillins of Skye; to the east, Ben More, the highest mountain on Mull; to the south, the Paps of Jura, while lying to the west is the lighthouse of Skerryvore, several miles off Tiree. Closer to the north lie the Treshnish Isles and the island of Staffa, famous for Fingal's Cave and its puffins, which is easily accessible from Iona and well worth a visit. Close to shore at the north end of the island is a small rise called 'the Hill of the Seat' (Cnoc an Suidne) where Columba is reputed to have sat in meditation. At the north-eastern tip of the island is 'the White Strand of the Monks' (Traigh Ban nam Monach) where on Christmas Eve 986 the abbot and fifteen monks were slaughtered by Viking raiders. These killings marked the end of the Viking attacks which had gone on intermittently since the end of the eighth century;

Iona, the holy island of peace, has experienced its own bloodshed and violence.

The path down Dun I is stony, but soon we strike pastureland and the homeward road. Shortly after rejoining this road we pass a granite cross erected by the Duke of Argyll in 1878 in memory of his wife. This monument is a silent reminder of the long connection between Iona and the Argyll estates.

In the biblical tradition, mountains and hills have been understood as places of vision and transfiguration. Here on the 'mountain top' we are reminded of one of George MacLeod's great prayers:

Invisible we see you, Christ above us,
With earthly eyes we see above us clouds or sunshine,
But with the eye of faith we know you reign:
instinct in the sun ray,
speaking in the storm,
warming and moving all creation,
Christ above us.
All is in flux; turn but a stone and an angel moves.
Underneath are the everlasting arms.
Unknowable we know you, Christ beneath us.

17

The Reilig Odhrain

In order to reach St Oran's Chapel, the final station of our pilgrimage, we have to walk through part of the ancient cemetery of Iona – the Reilig Odhrain or Oran's graveyard. Like the chapel, it is named after Odhrain, a cousin of Columba, who was reputedly the first of his companions to die and be buried on the island, although later monks were buried nearer the Abbey.

Between the ninth and eleventh centuries the Reilig Odhrain was a royal burial ground, although the actual number of kings buried on Iona has always been a matter of debate. It is usually said that forty-eight Scottish kings, eight Norwegian, four Irish and many Lords of the Isles rest here, but on Iona legend and fact are not easily disentangled, and the graveslabs themselves reveal no clear indication. It is widely held that both Duncan and Macbeth lie here, but we cannot be certain.

Adjoining the Reilig Odhrain is part of the medieval 'Street of the Dead' (Sraid nam Marbh) along which the funeral processions passed. It is an exceptionally fine example of a medieval paved roadway – truly a 'pilgrim way' connecting the graveyard with the Abbey.

Today, many of the magnificent graveslabs are not in the cemetery but are displayed in the museum and in the Cloisters. Along with the effigies and crosses, they constitute a truly rich treasury of medieval art, and the Cathedral Trustees are committed to the huge task of maintaining this priceless national heritage for future generations.

Adjacent to the old graveyard is a smaller, newer cemetery which is the burial place of local families. The gravestones here remind us not of the great figures of history about whom we often know little, but of the folk who have lived in the village in recent times. Their stories, although not recorded in our history books, are of equal interest to many of us who love this island. Here lie the women and men who have worked the land and fished the seas and welcomed many a stranger – the local villagers, without whom, Iona for all its world-wide fame, would be truly impoverished

Resurrection as our final and ultimate future can be known only by those who perceive resurrection with us now, encompassing all we are and do. For only then will it be recognized as a country we have already entered and in whose light and warmth we have already lived.

Harry Williams

Father and friend,
help us to learn that goodness is stronger than evil;
that love is stronger than hate;
that light is stronger than darkness;
that life is stronger than death;
that victory is ours
through your forgiving love.

Desmond Tutu

18

St Oran's Chapel

It is within these ancient walls that our pilgrimage ends, but every day for much of the year pilgrims gather in this, the oldest building on Iona. It dates from the twelfth century and may have been constructed as a family tomb for the MacDonalds, one of the ruling families of the time. In one historical account is a wonderful description of the funeral of John MacDonald, who was the first Lord of the Isles:

> The abbots and monks and vicars came to meet him, as was the custom to meet the King of the Hebrides, and his services and waking were honourably performed during eight days and eight nights and he was laid in the same grave with his father in the Church of Odhrain in the year of our Lord 1380.

However, in the following centuries the importance of the chapel gradually declined, and 300 years later, in 1688, one traveller described it simply as 'a decayed oratory'. By that date most of the ecclesiastical buildings on the island were also in a state of decay.

On a wintry day in 1925, Ina, Duchess of Argyll (whose effigy is in the Abbey church), was brought to Iona for burial. A photograph taken that day shows the villagers and estate workers carrying her coffin, and behind them we can see clearly a roofless St Oran's Chapel. Just over thirty years later, in 1957, the chapel was restored under the direction of the Scottish architect Ian G. Lindsay, who was a pivotal figure in the reconstruction of the Cloistral buildings.

A graveyard may seem an odd place to finish the Iona pilgrimage, but Christians have always celebrated the fact that it was in a burial place that the resurrection faith began.

St Oran's Chapel

It is often in places of death and apparent hopelessness that new beginnings are given to us by God. In this chapel our prayer is that, through the self-giving deaths of Oran and Columba, and the many other women and men of faith who have gone before us, we may be granted the strength and vision to continue on the journey of Jesus.

I ask God from the wealth of his glory to be strong in your inner selves, and I pray that Christ will make his home in your hearts through faith. I pray that you may have your roots and foundation in love, so that you, together with all God's people, may have the power to understand how broad and long, how high and deep is God's love – although it can never be fully known – and so be completely filled with the very nature of God.

Ephesians 3:16–19

May God's goodness be yours,
And well, and seven times well, may you spend your lives:
May you be an isle in the sea,
May you be a hill on the shore,
May you be a star in the darkness,
May you be a staff to the weak
And may the power of the Spirit
Pour on you, richly and generously,
Today, and in the days to come.

The Iona Community Worship Book

Journeying on...

For many pilgrims, new directions begin to take shape in their lives after they have left Iona. Back home, far from the rough paths and restless tides of the island, they find the Spirit opening up new and uncharted possibilities.

When God surprises us with such promptings it is at the same time both challenging and threatening. Do we listen to that inner voice or just go on as before?

Moving away from familiar landmarks is full of risk, and it needs courage and prayer to make the first step. Often the answers do not come quickly or with any clarity. We feel we are walking in a mist, and sometimes very much alone.

Yet as we look back to our Iona pilgrimage, we come to realize that we have many companions – all round the world – walking with us in prayer and in understanding friendship.

We are not alone as our heart seeks God's guidance – a thought which in itself is both comforting and restoring. The road is filled with pilgrims – laughing and crying and sharing stories, seeking the God who surprises us all.

✤

Bless to us, O God
The moon that is above us,
The earth that is beneath us,
The friends who are around us,
Your image deep within us.

Celtic traditional

May the road rise to meet you;
May the wind be always at your back;
May the rain fall softly upon your fields; May God hold
you in the hollow of his hand.

A Gaelic blessing

An island farewell

Further Reading

Argyll, *The Inventory of the Monuments: Volume 4: Iona*, The Royal Commission on the Ancient and Historical Monuments of Scotland, 1982.

Bradley, Ian, *Columba: Pilgrim and Penitent*, Wild Goose Publications, Glasgow, 1996.

De Waal, Esther, *The Celtic Vision: Prayers and Blessings from the Outer Hebrides*, Darton, Longmann & Todd, London, 1995.

MacArthur, E. Mairi, *Columba's Isle: Iona from Past to Present*, Edinburgh University Press, 1995.

Polhill, Chris, *A Pilgrim's Guide to Iona Abbey*, Wild Goose Publications, Glasgow, 2006.

Sheldrake, Philip, *Living Between Worlds: Place and Journey in Celtic Spirituality*, Darton, Longman & Todd, London, 1995.

The Iona Abbey Worship Book, Wild Goose Publications, Glasgow, 2001.

What is the Iona Community? Wild Goose Publications, Glasgow, 2000.